The Playboy of the Western World
Classroom Questions with Comparative Study

A SCENE BY SCENE TEACHING GUIDE

Amy Farrell

SCENE BY SCENE
ENNISKERRY, IRELAND

Copyright © 2017 by Scene by Scene.

Without limiting the rights under copyright, this book is sold subject to the condition that it shall not, by way of trade or otherwise be lent, resold, hired out, reproduced, stored on or introduced into a retrieval system, or transmitted, in any form or by any means (electronic, mechanical, photocopying, recording or otherwise), or otherwise circulated, without the publisher's prior consent, in any form other than that in which it is published and without a similar condition, including this condition, being imposed on the subsequent publisher.

All rights reserved. No part of this publication may be recorded or transmitted in any form or by any means electronic, mechanical, photocopying, recording or otherwise without the proper consent of the publisher.

The publisher reserves the right to change, without notice, at any time, the specification of this product, whether by change of materials, colours, format, text revision or any other characteristic.

Scene by Scene
Enniskerry
Wicklow, Ireland.
www.scenebysceneguides.com

The Playboy of the Western World Classroom Questions by Amy Farrell.
ISBN 978-1-910949-68-9

Contents

Act One	1
Act Two	15
Act Three	31
Further Questions	53
Theme/Issue (HL)/Relationships (OL)	56
Cultural Context (HL)/Social Setting (OL)	62
Literary Genre (HL)	68
General Vision and Viewpoint (HL)	74
Hero, Heroine, Villain (OL)	82
The Comparative Study: Comparing Texts	85

Act One

Summary

Pegeen Mike is writing a letter when Shawn Keogh comes into the shebeen, looking for her father.

Pegeen complains about being left home alone. Shawn says once they are married, she will not have to complain about that anymore.

They are waiting on a holy dispensation so they may marry. Pegeen says she would not bother with the likes of this place if she were the Holy Father.

Pegeen wonders how she will pass the night without dying of fear.

Shawn says he heard a man groaning in the ditch, but was too afraid to help him. He asks Pegeen not to tell her father or the men about it.

Michael James (Pegeen's father, also 'Michael' in the script), Philly Cutter and Jimmy Farrell come in and sit down.

Michael James asks Shawn if he is going to Kate Cassidy's wake, but he is not.

Pegeen scolds her father for taking off for the night. Michael James does not want to come home through the Stooks of the Dead Women, while Pegeen is fearful of being left at home alone all night.

When Jimmy tells her she has no-one to fear, she refers to the harvest boys, tinkers and militia as potential threats.

Michael James suggests that Shawn Keogh could stay with her, but he baulks at the idea, afraid of what Father Reilly and the Church would say.

Michael James wants him to stay because of the queer fellow above in the ditch.

Shawn is afraid of Father Reilly and does not want to be tempted by staying with Pegeen. He makes a big to-do and tries to run out, screaming at Michael James, calling him an old Pagan, while Michael James holds him by the coat-tails.

Shawn slips out of his coat and disappears out the door.

Michael James remarks that Shawn is a Christian man and that Pegeen need never spy on him, even with a score of young girls working for her.

Pegeen blames her father for not having a pot-boy to stay with her as she works.

Shawn puts his head in the door to tell Michael James he thinks the queer dying fellow has come to steal his hens. Shawn is afraid the man has heard what he has said about him.

Christy Mahon comes in and asks Pegeen for a glass of porter.

He asks if the police often visit the place, and satisfied that they do not, goes sighing and moaning to the fire, where he gnaws a turnip.

Michael James asks Christy if the police want him for larceny (theft).

When Christy denies this, Jimmy says he is wicked looking and may have followed a woman one lonesome night, something Christy also denies.

They quiz him, trying to discover his misdeed.

Pegeen says that he didn't do anything, that he is only saying it. She threatens to hit him with the broom. Scared, Christy tells them that he killed his father.

The others are impressed. Christy says his father was dirty and old, and he could not put up with him.

He hit his father in the head with a spade before burying him in the field where he was digging spuds.

That was eleven days ago and the police are not after him yet.

The others are impressed with Christy. Pegeen suggests he would make a good pot-boy.

Philly and Jimmy are impressed by his bravery. Michael James offers him a job.

Shawn is the only one to object to Christy. He thinks it odd to bring such a man into Pegeen Mike's household.

Pegeen shushes Shawn and her and Michael James convince Christy to stay. Jimmy says Pegeen will be safe now while they go to the wake.

Shawn offers to stay too, but Pegeen sends him on his way.

Pegeen flatters Christy, admiring his small feet and his quality name. She says he is a fine, handsome young fellow with a noble brow.

She comments that he must have heard the same said by all the girls he encounters, but he dismisses the notion. He says he has not told anyone his story until tonight.

He asks if she is single and she says she is.

Pegeen says she would be afraid to kill her father, unlike Christy. She wonders that his father was not afraid of him.

Christy says that until the day he did it, nobody knew what sort of a man he was.

Pegeen says girls must have paid heed to him, but he says nobody at home heeded him. He describes working all day, with his only fun being to poach rabbits at night.

Christy describes his father as a difficult drunkard. His only respite came when his father was locked up for battering peelers (police) or assaulting men. Pegeen assures him that he will have peace now. He says it is time he did, and he a seemly fellow with strength and bravery.

A knock at the door alarms Christy. He is afraid of the police and the walking dead. The Widow Quin is at the door.

Pegeen tells Christy to act sleepy or the Widow Quin will keep him talking all night.

The Widow Quin has come in case Christy was roaring with drink. She has promised Shawn Keogh and Father Reilly that Christy will lodge with her.

Pegeen tells the Widow Quin to leave. She replies that she will leave with Christy.

Christy asks the widow if she killed her father. Pegeen says she did not, that she hit her husband with a worn pick and he died from blood poisoning.

The Widow Quin says that a widow who buried her children and destroyed her man is more fitting company for Christy than a girl like Pegeen Mike.

The widow says there is great temptation in a man who killed his father. She tells him to get up.

Pegeen takes Christy's arm, saying he is the pot-boy and is not going anywhere.

Pegeen says he will see how tumbledown the widow's house is in the morning.

The widow counters that he will swear she was made for living alone when he sees what she can do.

Pegeen insults the Widow Quin, saying amongst other things, that she reared a ram at her breast.
The Widow Quin is amused by this and remarks to Christy that this is how Pegeen will speak to him after a week.

Pegeen tells Christy to tell the Widow Quin to go. The widow says she is going, but that Christy is going with her. He says he would prefer to stay.

The Widow Quin says that if he will not go, maybe she will stay too. Pegeen tells her to get out. The widow gathers herself to leave, but first warns Christy of the torment he will face if he romances Pegeen, and her waiting on a parchment so that she can marry Shawn Keogh.

Pegeen bolts the door and says she has no intention of marrying Shawn Keogh. She gives out about Shawn sending the widow to spy on her and bids Christy goodnight.

He settles under his quilt, commenting on his good luck to have two women fighting over him, saying he was a fool not to have killed his father before now.

Questions

1. What do you learn about the setting from the stage directions as this act begins?
   When is this story taking place?

2. What is Pegeen doing as the play begins?

3. Why has Shawn Keogh come to the pub?
   Is he happy to be alone with Pegeen?

4. Where is Michael James?

5. Shawn remarks to Pegeen that they will soon be married. What is your response to this?
   What is her response to this?

6. What is holding up their wedding?
   What does this mean?

7. Is Pegeen eager to marry Shawn?
   Support your answer with reference to the text.

8. Does Pegeen like living here?

9. What did Daneen Sullivan and Marcus Quinn do?
   How does this shape your impression of this place?

10. Why is Pegeen concerned about how she will pass the night?
    How does this affect the atmosphere?

11. Why doesn't Pegeen want Shawn to fetch the Widow Quin?

12. What is in the "furzy ditch"?
    What is your response to this?

13. What stopped Shawn from helping this man?
    What does this tell you about Shawn?

14. What does Pegeen point out about Shawn's behaviour here?
    What is Shawn's response?

15. What does Pegeen's behaviour reveal to you about her attitude to Shawn as the play begins?

16. How do the men greet Pegeen when they come in?
    What does this tell you about the setting?

17. What are your first impressions of Pegeen's relationship with her father, Michael James?
    Do they get on well together?

18. What do the references to "the Stooks of the Dead Women" and "dogs barking, and the calves mooing, and my own teeth rattling with fear" tell you about these characters, their world and beliefs?
    Do people have these same fears today?

19. What, exactly, is Pegeen afraid of?

20. Why doesn't Shawn want to stay with Pegeen?
What is your response to this?

21. Why does Michael James want Shawn to stay?

22. According to Michael James, who is in the ditch?
What is your response to this?
Are you surprised that nobody is investigating what is going on here?

23. Why does Shawn run from the shebeen?
What does this tell you about Shawn?
What does this tell you about this world?

24. How does Michael James respond to Shawn's departure?

25. Why does Shawn stick his head back in the door?

26. Is Shawn a very fearful character, in your view?

27. How do the others respond to Christy's arrival?

28. What question does Christy ask Michael James?
What does this tell the audience?

29. How is Christy behaving?
What effect would this have on the audience, do you think?

30. What crime does Michael James presume Christy is guilty of?

31. What other crimes do they suggest?

32. Do they treat Christy like a criminal here?

33. How does Pegeen get Christy to reveal his crime?

34. What motive did Christy have for committing this crime?
    What does this tell you about Christy?
    What does this tell you about the world of the play?

35. How do the others respond to learning of Christy's crime?
    What is your response to this?

36. What did Jimmy Farrell do to his dog?
    What is your response to this?

37. How did Christy kill his father?
    What is your response to this?

38. Why wasn't Christy hanged immediately after committing this crime?

39. Are you surprised that Christy has not been caught yet?

40. What effect does Christy's story have on the others?

41. Are you surprised that Michael James offers Christy the job of pot-boy?
    Give a reason for your answer.

42. How does Shawn react to this job offer?
    Why doesn't he respond like the others?

43. "Now, by the grace of God, herself will be safe this night, with a man killed his father holding danger from the

door..."
How do the locals view Christy?
What is your response to their view of Christy?

44. Michael James offers Christy a job before he asks him his name.
Comment on this.

45. Shawn tells Pegeen that he can stay too.
How does she respond to this offer?

46. What does Pegeen say that suggests she admires or fancies Christy?
What is your response to this?

47. Is Christy interested in Pegeen?
How do you know?

48. How does Pegeen feel about Christy killing his father?
Does she admire him for it?
If so, why?

49. What was life like for Christy at home?
What is your response to this?

50. Would you like a life like the one Christy describes?
Give a reason for your answer.

51. What sort of man was Christy's father, based on what Christy says here?

52. Do you feel sorry for Christy at all?

53. Do you blame him for killing his father?

54. How does Christy react to the knock at the door? Explain his reaction.

55. How would you be feeling, if you were Christy?

56. Who is at the door?
How does Pegeen Mike greet the visitor?

57. Why has the Widow Quin come to the shebeen?

58. What are the Widow Quin's first impressions of Christy?

59. How did the Widow Quin kill her husband?
What is your response to this?

60. Why do they argue over where Christy will spend the night?
What is your response to this?

61. "There's great temptation in a man did slay his da."
Explain this line and the reasoning behind Christy going to stay with the Widow Quin.
What insight does this give you into the world of the play?

62. What does Pegeen say to try to insult the Widow Quin?
What is your response to these insults?

63. How does the Widow Quin react to Pegeen Mike's insulting comments?

64. What makes this scene entertaining?
    Include examples in your answer.

65. How does the Widow Quin respond to Christy saying he will stay in the shebeen?
    Why is she doing this?
    What is your response to this?

66. Why does the Widow Quin tell Christy that Pegeen Mike is to marry Shawn Keogh?

67. How does Pegeen react to the widow's words?

68. What does Pegeen Mike think of Shawn Keogh?

69. Does Pegeen intend to marry Shawn Keogh?
    Would you, in her position?

70. Read Christy's speech as the act ends.
    What is your response to his words here?

71. What are your impressions of this story after Act One?

72. Is this an amusing or serious opening act?
    Refer to examples in the play to support the points you make.

73. How do the others view Christy when he tells them he is a murderer?
    What is your response to this?

74. What are your impressions of Pegeen, Shawn, Michael James, Christy and the Widow Quin after the first act? Include examples to support your point of view.

75. Does the Widow Quin's killing of her husband add a dark note to this story?
Why, do you think, is she walking free?
What does this suggest about this place?

76. Is Shawn Keogh a good representation of a devout Christian?
Is there anything problematic about the way he is portrayed?

77. Now that you have got to know a little about these characters and their world, what strikes you about their outlook and values?

78. What view of murder do these characters have? Comment on their outlook and what it suggests about their lives.

79. What, do you think, will happen next?

Act Two

Summary

Act Two begins with Christy cleaning Pegeen Mike's boots as he counts the crockery on the dresser.

He talks about what a good place this would be to live, compared to his home.

Looking out the window he sees girls he does not know, so he goes into the other room to dress.

Susan, Nelly, Honor and Sara enter the shebeen, looking for the man Shawn Keogh told them about. They are keen to meet this man who murdered his father.

Sara calls him into the room and he meekly enters. They have each brought him a gift of food. The Widow Quin arrives and sets them to preparing Christy's breakfast.

She asks Christy to tell them his story before Pegeen comes back.

Christy says it is a long story, but is enjoying being asked to divulge his tale.

The Widow Quin asks where it happened, and if Christy had wanted money from his father, or had intended getting a wife and putting his father off the farm.

Christy says his father wanted him to marry fat, old, Widow Casey, because he was after her home and money.

The women encourage Christy to recount the argument he had with his father, ending with him striking him in the head with a spade.
The girls find the story wonderful.

Susan suggests that God has sent Christy to marry the Widow Quin. Sara fetches porter so Christy and the Widow Quin can drink a toast together.

Pegeen Mike comes in with a milkcan and stands aghast. Angrily, she asks first Sara and then the Widow Quin what they want.

The Widow Quin calls Pegeen mighty huffy and leaves with the girls.

Pegeen tells Christy to tidy up, which he does.

He remarks that it is a fine country for young, lovely girls. Pegeen tells him to stop his talk of lovely girls.

Christy takes up a loy (spade) and tells her it is the same one he killed his father with. He is trying to impress her.

Pegeen says she has heard the story six times since daybreak.

Christy says it is odd she does not want to hear his story when the girls walked four miles to hear it.

Pegeen says they did not walk nearly so far.

She tells him she was down looking at the papers this morning and there is great news. She talks about a report of a man's hanging, saying it is the type of end for a man who destroyed his da.

Christy worries whether he is safe, looking for reassurance from Pegeen Mike.

She tells him he will not be safe if he talks to the likes of the girls, who talk to the police.

Christy is scared and suggests maybe he better get going. Pegeen plays with him, telling him maybe he should.

He says it is a poor thing for him, a lonesome fellow, to be starting again. They talk about lonesomeness, with Pegeen not believing that Christy could be lonesome and all the girls around.

He insists he was lonesome, puzzling Pegeen.

He tells her his heart is scalded as he turns to go.

Pegeen says he is the pot-boy now and cannot mitch off work.

He reminds her that she said he had better go.

She tells him that she has been down and read the last few weeks' newspapers, and there is no mention of the murder in them.

Christy realises she was playing with him, and is happy to stay with her.

The Widow Quin arrives with Shawn Keogh. Shawn tells Pegeen her sheep are eating cabbages in Jimmy's field and she runs out.

Christy is about to go and help her when the Widow Quin stops him. Shawn wants to talk to Christy.

Shawn offers Christy half a ticket to the Western States, his new hat, his breeches, his new coat, and his blessing, along with the blessing of Father Reilly, if he will leave.

Shawn does not want Christy living in Pegeen's house when Shawn is going to marry her. He tells Christy he would be beter off beyond.

The Widow Quin joins in with Shawn, saying Christy should leave and not have Pegeen setting her mind on him, even though everyone is saying she will marry him.

Shawn insists that Pegeen would not suit Christy, that they would be strangling each other in no time. He thinks a quiet man like him would be a much better match for Pegeen.

The Widow Quin tells Christy to try on Shawn's offered clothes. He agrees, as he would like Pegeen to see him dressed in them. He goes to get changed.

Shawn does not think Christy will leave. The Widow Quin jeers Shawn that it is true that all girls like courage and so hate the like of him.

Shawn is too scared to turn Christy in or kill him. He asks the Widow Quin for help, reminding her that he will give her a ewe if she helps him.

The Widow Quin asks what he would give her if she married Christy.

She asks for his red cow, mountainy ram, a right of way across his rye path, a load of dung at Michaelmas and turbary (the right to cut turf) on the western hill, in exchange for this match.

He agrees, also offering his wedding ring, the loan of a suit, two kids (young goats) for the dinner, a gallon of poteen and a piper for the wedding.

Christy comes back in, dressed in Shawn's finery. Shawn says he can borrow the clothes to wear to the sports, and leaves.

Christy wants to go and find Pegeen, but the Widow Quin tells him to sit and talk with her.

Christy is full of swagger as he goes to the door. He opens it to see his murdered father (called 'Mahon' and 'Old Mahon' in the script). Christy hides behind the door as Mahon walks in.

Mahon asks the Widow Quin if she saw a young lad pass this way.

She remarks that he is a queer fellow to walk in without any greeting.

He asks again if she saw the young lad. He wants him for breaking his head with a loy. He shows her his bandaged head. Mahon says his own son did it, no robber, but a dirty, stuttering lout.

The Widow Quin says he must have vexed his son for him to strike his father.

Mahon says his lazy son has him destroyed. He reels off a list of Christy's flaws for the Widow Quin, calling him the laughing joke of every female where four baronies meet.

Mahon describes his son as a small, low fellow, dark and dirty. The Widow Quin says she thinks she saw him, that he has gone over the hills. She points out a shortcut for him to take and Mahon leaves abruptly.

Christy is worried about what Pegeen will say once she hears the truth.

The Widow Quin says Pegeen will throw him out, seeing as he made up the murder.

Christy is very angry that his father pretended to be dead and followed him like this. Christy curses his father, shocking the Widow Quin. He tells her that now Pegeen will turn against him, when things have been going so well between them. He wonders what he will do now.

The Widow Quin tells him he will be doing the same as her.

Christy is interested to hear how she is like him. The Widow Quin tells him he could live with her and she would look after him.

Voices outside call for Christy.

He asks the Widow Quin to help him win Pegeen, as his heart is set on her. Christy says he will pray for her in her hour of death if she helps him.

She asks if he will give her a right of way she wants, a mountainy ram and a load of dung at Michaelmas once he is master there. He agrees. The Widow Quin says they will not mention the old fellow to Pegeen. If he turns up again, they will swear he is a maniac and not Christy's da.

The girls come in, wanting Christy to go to the sports with them. They say Pegeen is in the boreen, making fun of Shaneen Keogh, so he goes with them.

The widow speaks to an empty stage, saying if the worst comes, it will be great game to see there is no-one to pity him, but the likes of her.

Questions

1. What is Christy doing as the act begins?
   What is the significance of this?

2. Why would Christy prefer to live here than his old home?

3. What makes Christy go and hide?

4. Why have the girls come to the shebeen?

5. Where is Pegeen Mike?

6. What have the girls brought Christy?
   What is your reaction to this?

7. What does the Widow Quin do when she arrives?

8. Is Christy enjoying himself, do you think?
   Give reasons for your answer.

9. What suggestions does the Widow Quin make about Christy's reasons to kill his father?
   What does this tell you about the Widow Quin?

10. What was the cause of the disagreement that day?
    Does this surprise you?

11. How does Christy describe the Widow Casey?

12. Why did Christy's father suggest this match?
    What is your response to this?

13. Describe the argument Christy and his father had.
    Was it very heated?

14. How has Christy's explanation of why he killed his father changed since the night before?
    Can you explain this change?

15. Are the women impressed with Christy's story?
    What is your response to this?

16. What has God sent Christy for, according to Susan?
    Why might this be the case?

17. Comment on the toast Christy and the Widow Quin drink to.

18. What disrupts this scene?

19. How does Pegeen treat the other women?
    What makes her behave this way?
    Can you really blame her for her reaction here or is it understandable?

20. Why can't Sara buy her tobacco?
    Is tobacco really the reason why she came here?

21. Why won't Pegeen Mike sell starch to the Widow Quin?

22. Why is Pegeen Mike so annoyed?
    How would you feel in her position?

23. Why does Christy take up a loy?
    How does Pegeen Mike respond?

24. What "great news" does Pegeen have?

25. According to Pegeen, how would a man that destroyed his da be buried?
What makes her say this to Christy?

26. What does Pegeen say to make Christy distrust the girls who were just in?

27. The stage directions tell us that Pegeen Mike is beginning to play with Christy here.
What does this mean?
Why is she doing this, do you think?

28. Why does Christy call himself a "lonesome fellow"?
Does he sound lonesome to you?

29. Why isn't Pegeen lonesome, according to Christy?

30. Does Pegeen believe that Christy is lonesome?

31. Why, do you think, does Pegeen admire Christy?

32. How does Christy feel about Pegeen?
Refer to the text to support your view.

33. How does Pegeen react when Christy says he is leaving?

34. Comment on the relationship that is developing between Pegeen Mike and Christy Mahon.

35. How does Pegeen reassure Christy that he is safe, staying with her?

36. How does Christy feel about staying with Pegeen?

37. What makes Pegeen leave the shebeen?

38. Why does the Widow Quin stop Christy from going after Pegeen?
    What is your response to this?

39. What does Shawn offer Christy?

40. Why is he making him this offer?
    What is your response to this offer?

41. What does Shawn say to make "beyond" sound attractive?

42. What reason to leave does the Widow Quin give Christy?
    How does he respond to her comments?

43. Why wouldn't Pegeen suit Christy, according to Shawn?
    What makes him say this?
    Is there any truth in this, do you think?

44. Would you want to leave if you were Christy?
    Give reasons for your answer.

45. Why does the Widow Quin tell Christy to dress in Shawn's clothes?

46. What insulting remark does the Widow Quin make to Shawn?
    Why does she say this, do you think?

47. What is stopping Shawn from turning Christy in?

48. What is stopping Shawn from killing Christy?

49. What has Shawn promised the Widow Quin if she helps him?

50. What sort of person is Shawn, based on what we have seen so far?
Use examples to support your point of view.

51. What solution does the Widow Quin offer Shawn?
What is your response to this?

52. What proposal does she offer Shawn?
What is your response to this bargain?

53. What else will Shawn give her if she weds Christy?
What does this tell you about Shawn?

54. Why does Christy want to go and find Pegeen while wearing Shawn's clothes?
What does this tell you about Christy?

55. Is there anything significant or symbolic in Christy's new outfit?
Explain your point of view fully.

56. The stage directions tell us Christy "swaggers to the door." What makes him act this way?

57. What does Christy see when he opens the door?
    How does he react?
    What is your response to this?
    What makes this an exciting moment in the play?

58. How does Mahon speak to the Widow Quin?
    What does this tell you about him?

59. Why has Mahon come to the shebeen?
    What does this mean for Christy?

60. How do you know that this man is Christy's 'murdered' father?

61. How does Mahon describe Christy to the Widow Quin?
    How must Christy feel, listening to this description of himself?

62. Mahon tells the Widow Quin that Christy cannot drink or smoke and is a laughing stock with the local women. Why, do you think, does he focus on these aspects of Christy's character?
    What does this tell you about this world?

63. Does Mahon's description of Christy match what you have seen of him so far?
    Comment on Mahon's view of his son.

64. Where does the Widow Quin tell him his son is?
    Why does she say this?

65. Once Mahon leaves, the Widow Quin calls Christy "the walking Playboy of the Western World."
What does she mean by this?

66. What is Christy's first concern, once his father leaves?
What is your response to this?

67. How will Pegeen react when she learns the truth, according to the Widow Quin?
What makes her say this, do you think?
How will Pegeen react if she hears the truth, in your opinion?

68. How does Christy feel about his father being alive?
What does this tell you about Christy?
What does this tell you about Christy's relationship with his father?

69. What does Christy say about his father that shocks the Widow Quin?
Why does he speak this way about him?

70. Does the Widow Quin share Christy's high opinion of Pegeen Mike?

71. Christy wonders what he will do when Pegeen loses interest in him.
What answer does the Widow Quin have for him?
What is your response to this?

72. Is Christy won over by the Widow Quin?
How does this affect your view of Christy?

73. What will Christy do for the Widow Quin if she helps him?
    Comment on this.

74. What bargain does the Widow Quin strike with Christy?
    What is your response to this?

75. How will the Widow Quin help Christy?
    Does she surprise you here?
    What does this promise of help tell you about her?

76. Why do the girls come to the shebeen?

77. Comment on the Widow Quin's final words as this act closes.

78. What is the atmosphere like at this point?

79. Is a lot at stake for the characters?
    Explain your view.

80. Does Christy's attitude towards his father affect how you feel about Christy?
    Explain your viewpoint.

81. Will Pegeen Mike and Christy get together, do you think?
    Give a reason for your answer.

82. What type of person is the Widow Quin?
    How does her character add to the story?

83. How do you expect this story to end? Give reasons for your answer.

Act Three

Summary

It is later the same day. Jimmy comes in, slightly drunk, calling for Pegeen. Philly looks for a drink, but the cupboards are locked. Jimmy wonders at Pegeen being so fussy, after all that Christy has won in the sports.

Philly says Christy cannot say ten words without bragging about killing his father. Philly wonders what will happen when Mahon's skull is discovered in the field.

As the men talk about skulls and bones, Mahon comes in and sits down. Mahon shows them his head and tells them his son did it to him. He asks them for a drink.

The Widow Quin comes in, shocked to see Mahon. She sits down and gives him a glass of poteen.

She tells the men that she has seen this man before. She says he is raving from his wound, that he said a tinker inflicted on him, when she saw him before. She claims he heard Christy's tale and has mixed himself into it. Jimmy believes her, but Philly asks whether Mahon saw Christy. The Widow Quin warns him not to mention him.

She goes over and talks to Mahon. He says he is poorly because of the way he is today, after caring for his son for years.

She asks him if his son was 'a great hand at racing and lepping and licking the world.'

He roars at her that his son is a fool.

They hear cheers outside from the racing.

Mahon looks at the 'playboy' they told him about and says if the man were a fool, he would be a great likeness for his son.

Mahon decides to walk down to see the race, but the Widow Quin stops him.

They sit and watch the race, which Christy wins despite a fall.

Christy is raised aloft, at which point his father recognises him and roars with rage and astonishment. He makes a run for the door, but the Widow Quin holds him back.

Jimmy holds Mahon while the Widow Quin shakes him and tells him the man he sees is not his son, but the man who is going to marry the daughter of the house they are in.

When Mahon hears that Christy is about to marry a decent girl with money, he wonders if he is in the crazy house. He gets distressed, wondering if he is going mad.

The widow says it is no wonder, considering his head injury.

Mahon says he has never been mad before, not even when drinking for three weeks with the Limerick girls.

He gets up and says he will go to the union (workhouse).

The Widow Quin tells him to be hasty, for one time the lads chased a maniac into the sea, where he drowned.

Mahon heeds her and runs off down the boreen.

Philly says he will go after Mahon and give him some dinner and let him rest, before he decides he is mad. Jimmy follows Philly.

Some others come in with Christy and Pegeen. They give Christy his prizes and head out to a tug-of-war, leaving Christy and Pegeen alone inside.

Christy asks Pegeen to marry him in a fortnight. At first she appears reluctant, saying he will be returning to some girl at home when his father is rotten in four or five months time.

Christy insists he will do no such thing. He describes how they will be together. Pegeen Mike wonders how Christy Mahon, with his poetic words, has fallen for her. They are thrilled by the idea of being together.

Drunken singing is heard as Michael James returns. Pegeen says they will tell her father their plan to marry once he has had a sleep.

Michael James comes in and criticises Christy for not giving his father a Christian burial.

He has received a special dispensation and intends to marry Pegeen Mike to

Shawn Keogh right away.

Pegeen says the dispensation has come too late, that she is marrying Christy Mahon.

Michael James is horrified at the idea of being related to a father murderer.

Pegeen says she will marry Christy, not dull Shawn.

Michael James is distraught that Pegeen will wed Christy. He asks Shawn if he has anything to say to help him, but Shawn is too afraid to be jealous of a murderer.

Pegeen is glad not to have married Shawn already.

Shawn says it is strange for her to pick a dirty tramp and asks if she has no concern for his passion, the holy dispensation and his money.

Pegeen replies that he is too fine for the likes of her.

Christy tells Shawn to leave before he commits another murder.

Michael James tells them to go down to the beach if they want to fight and pushes Shawn towards Christy. Shawn gets behind Michael James and tells Michael James to strike him. Michael James pushes Shawn and tells him to fight Christy. Shawn wonders whether to strike Christy. Michael James tells him to use the loy, but Shawn is afraid he will be hanged if he hits Christy with it.

Christy takes up the loy and Shawn runs out the door.
Christy turns to Michael James and tells him he will be better off without

Shawn in his house. He asks Michael James for his blessing, as does Pegeen.

Michael James says he would rather face an untimely death with a score of grandsons growing up to be gallant swearers, than see the puny weeds Shaneen Keogh would father. He adds that a man daring enough to kill his father is brave indeed, and gives them his blessing.

Mahon runs in and attacks Christy.

Pegeen calls Christy a liar for saying he killed his father when the man lives. Christy says Mahon is not his father, turning to the Widow Quin for help. The crowd call Christy a liar. Christy says Mahon is the liar, for pretending to be dead.

Pegeen tells Christy to leave. She is annoyed that she had her heart set on him.

Mahon tells Christy to come with him.

The crowd jeers Christy.

Christy appeals to the widow for protection, but she says she has done what she can.

Christy asks if he must return to his torment.

Pegeen tells Mahon to take him out or she will set the young lads on him.

Mahon tells him to go and shakes his stick at him, but Christy resists.

The crowd are eager for a fight.

Christy grabs a loy and chases his father outside. Noise, a yell, and silence follows. Christy comes back in.

The Widow Quin tells him they are turning against him and to get a move on before he is hanged.

Christy thinks that now Pegeen will praise him, as she did before.

The Widow Quin tells him to get going, but he insists he will not leave Pegeen. Sara rushes in saying they are going to hang Christy. She offers him a disguise to flee in, but he says he will stay. He accuses the Widow Quin of being jealous over his wedding.

The Widow Quin says it is the madhouse, not the jail they should put Christy in. She leaves with Sara, by the back door, to fetch a doctor and so save Christy.

The men come in with a rope. They discuss who should put it around Christy's neck. Shawn tells Pegeen Mike to do it, which she does. Shawn says they will take Christy to the police for hanging.

Christy refuses to go. He asks Pegeen what she has to say to him after everyone seeing him do it this time.

She says she has learned the great difference between a bold story and a dirty deed. She tells the men to take him or they will all end up on trial.

Christy is horrified that Pegeen will send him to the hangman. The men pull on the rope and Christy is pulled to the floor. He twists his arms round the table and asks Pegeen to cut the rope, saying he will leave them all and live like the madman of Keel if she does.

She tells the men to get him out. Shawn is afraid of getting too near Christy. He tells Pegeen to scorch Christy's leg to make him let go of the table.

Pegeen works the bellows, telling Christy to let go or she will scorch him. Christy says she is trying to torture him. He warns them all that he will shed some of their blood before he dies. Shawn is afraid of Christy.

Christy imagines how upset the ladies in Mayo will be the day he is hanged.

Christy squirms on the floor and bites Shawn's leg, making him shriek.

Mahon crawls in the door, unnoticed.

The men tell Pegeen to bring the sod and she burns Christy's leg. He releases the table and is dragged towards the door.

Jimmy sees Mahon. The men drop Christy and run. Christy scrambles on his knees to face his father and asks if he has come to be killed a third time.

Mahon asks what is going on and Christy explains that they are taking him to be hanged for slaying his father.

Michael James says everyone has to guard their home from the treachery of the law and asks what would become of Pegeen if he were ruined or hanged.

Mahon says he is leaving with his son. He says they will speak of the villainy and fools of Mayo in future. Christy says his father will tend to him and he will be the master from now on. Mahon praises God and declares he is crazy again as he goes out the door.

Christy blesses them all before leaving for turning him into a 'likely gaffer' who will romp through life.

Once they leave, Michael James asks Pegeen to pour the porter. Shawn tells her it is a miracle that they can wed.

Pegeen boxes him on the ear and breaks down with grief, having lost the only Playboy of the Western World.

Questions

1. Why has Philly sent Shawn Keogh with the asscart?

2. What makes Jimmy say that Christy has "right luck"?
   Why is it significant that Christy is a 'winner'?

3. Chrity knows his father lives, yet he continues to brag about his murder.
   What is your response to this?
   What does this tell you about Christy?

4. What starts Philly and Jimmy talking about skulls and bones?
   How does this imagery affect the atmosphere?

5. Why is it significant that Mahon comes in and sits down as the men talk?

6. What does Mahon tell Philly and Jimmy?
   How do they respond?
   Why do they respond this way?

7. How does the Widow Quin react when she sees Mahon?

8. What story does the Widow Quin tell Jimmy and Philly about Mahon and his wound?
   What is your response to her lie?

9. Do the men believe the Widow Quin's story about Mahon, do you think?
   Give a reason for your answer.

10. What does Mahon talk to the Widow Quin about?

11. What question does the Widow Quin ask Mahon about his son?
    Why does she phrase it this way?

12. How does he answer her question?
    What is your response to this?

13. How does the Widow Quin describe Christy to Mahon?

14. What does Mahon say when he sees Christy mounted on the horse?
    Is this a tense moment?
    Explain your point of view.

15. Why does Mahon want to watch the race, do you think?

16. Does the race sound exciting?
    Give a reason for your answer.

17. When does Mahon recognise his son?
    How does he react?
    How would you feel, in his position?
    What makes this an exciting moment in the play?

18. What does the Widow Quin say to make Jimmy hold Mahon?
    How do her words affect the atmosphere?

19. What, do you think, does Mahon want to do to Christy?
    Would you feel the same way, if you were him?

20. How does Mahon react to the news of Christy's imminent marriage?
    What does this suggest about how he views his son?

21. How must the audience feel at this point?
    What, do you think, will happen next?

22. "Aren't you after saying that your son's a fool, and how would they be cheering a true born idiot?"
    Explain the conflict of identity here.

23. Why does Mahon get distressed as he hears the cheering?

24. What 'visions' has Mahon had in the past?
    Comment on the imagery here.

25. How do these 'visions' affect the audience's opinion of Mahon?

26. What did Mahon do with the Limerick girls?
    How does this detail add to your view of the man?

27. Why does Mahon feel he will be welcomed into the workhouse (the union)?

28. How do these references to drink and the workhouse affect your view of Mahon's relationship with his son?

29. According to the Widow Quin, how did the lads treat a maniac they caught one time?
    Why is she telling him this?
    What does this tell you about the society of the play?

30. Does the Widow Quin do a good job of manipulating Mahon in this scene?
    Use examples from the text to support your ideas.

31. Is Philly convinced by the Widow Quin?

32. Why does Jimmy go after Philly?

33. What is the mood like as the others come in?

34. How has Christy got on in the sports?

35. What does Christy ask Pegeen?

36. What stops her from agreeing at once?

37. How does Christy describe their future life together?
    Does this sound appealing to you?

38. What does Pegeen like about Christy?

39. What does Christy like about Pegeen?

40. Is this a tender moment in the play?
    If so, what makes it tender?

41. How do Pegeen and Christy feel about getting married and being together?
    Does this sound romantic to you?

42. How does Michael James greet Christy when he sees him?

43. What does Michael James's comment about men "stretched and retching speechless on the holy stones" mean?

44. Why does Michael James criticise Christy? Is this criticism fair or unfair in your view? What does it tell you about this world?

45. How has the mood changed with Michael James's arrival?

46. What "gilded dispensation" has Michael James received? What does this mean for Pegeen Mike?

47. What differences do you notice in the way Michael James speaks about Christy, compared to the other villagers? Can you explain this differing viewpoint?

48. How does Michael James react to Pegeen's statement that she will marry Christy? What makes him feel this way? Are you surprised by his reaction here?

49. How does Pegeen speak about Shawn? Is her view of him fair, in your view?

50. What stops Shawn from speaking up for himself? What is your response to this?

51. Pegeen is glad not to have married Shawn already. Would you have the same outlook, if you were her?

52. What does Shawn mention to try to change her mind?

53. How does Christy threaten Shawn?

54. Why won't Shawn fight Christy?

55. Why won't Michael James fight Christy?

56. Why does Shawn fly out the door?

57. Were you anticipating a violent turn of events? Why/why not?

58. What does Christy ask Michael James for?
What does this tell you about this world?

59. Why does Michael James give Pegeen and Christy his blessing?
Has he been won over too easily, in your view?

60. If you were Pegeen Mike's father, who would you wish her to marry?
Give reasons to support your answer.

61. How do things change once Mahon appears?
Do Christy and Pegeen get to enjoy their engagement?

62. How does Pegeen react to learning that Christy's father is alive?
What is your response to this?

63. What stops the Widow Quin from coming to Christy's defence?

64. Why does Christy call his father a liar?
    What is your response to this?

65. Pegeen tells Christy to "Quit off from this."
    What does this mean?
    What makes her say this?
    Are you surprised by her here?
    Is she entitled to feel this way?

66. What does Mahon tell Christy to do?
    What does this mean?

67. How do the crowd treat Christy?
    Can you explain this treatment?

68. What does Christy's future hold?

69. Pegeen is on the verge of tears when she tells Mahon to take Christy out or she will "set the young lads to destroy him here."
    Why is she upset?
    Why does she threaten Christy this way?
    Can you explain her behaviour here?

70. Pegeen calls Christy, "an ugly liar was playing off the hero."
    What is your response to her words?

71. How does Christy react to his changing circumstances?
    How would you feel, if you were him?

72. Christy chases his father out of the pub with a loy in his hand.
    What is the atmosphere like at this point?
    What is motivating Christy here?
    What is your response to this?

73. The stage directions tell us there is noise outside, then a yell, and then silence.
    What has happened here?
    What is your response to this development?
    Will his actions here make the locals admire Christy again, do you think?
    Give a reason for your answer.

74. Why is the Widow Quin anxious for Christy to leave?

75. The Widow Quin says now Christy will have a double murder to tell the girls about.
    Explain her comment.
    Is it funny in this context, do you think?

76. Why does Christy insist on staying?

77. What news does Sara bring when she comes in?
    Does this surprise you?
    Why have things changed so much for Christy?

78. What disguise does Sara offer for Christy?

79. Where will the Widow Quin take him?
    Is he lucky to have her on his side?

80. Why does Christy still want to stay, even with the threat of hanging?
    Does he fully comprehend what is going on, do you think?

81. Why do the Widow Quin and Sara go for the doctor?
    Does the Widow Quin care about Christy, do you think?

82. Why do the Widow Quin and Sara leave by the back door?

83. What makes this a tense moment in the play?
    Be specific in your answer.

84. What question does Michael James ask when he comes in?
    Why is this significant?

85. What is Michael James carrying?
    What does this tell the audience?

86. Are the men eager or reluctant to approach Christy?
    How do you know?
    How does this add to the scene?

87. How does Pegeen Mike respond when Shawn tells her to take the rope?
    What is your response to this?

88. What does Shawn plan to do with Christy?
    What is your response to this?

89. Comment on the collective actions of the villagers here.
    Is Christy being treated fairly?
    Is this real justice?

90. Can you explain why the locals have turned on Christy?

91. What does Pegeen Mike say to Christy, now that he has completed his father's murder?
    What is your response to this?
    Do you feel sorry for Christy?

92. Comment on the action here as Christy is pulled onto the floor and twists his arms around the table.
    How is he being treated?
    How would you feel if you were in the audience?
    What, exactly, is the audience witnessing?

93. What does Christy promise Pegeen if she will cut the rope around his neck?
    Comment on the imagery here.
    Does this remind you of any other character you have come across?
    Why doesn't she do as he asks?

94. Can you explain why Pegeen has turned on Christy?
    What is your view of the way she treats him here?

95. What method does Shawn suggest to make Christy let go of the table?
    What is your response to this?

CLASSROOM QUESTIONS • 49

96. What does Christy warn the others he will do before he is hanged?
What is your response to these threats?
Would you make similar threats, in his position?
Explain your point of view.

97. How does Christy imagine the day he will be "stretched upon the rope"?
Is this in keeping with his character?

98. Why does Christy bite Shawn's leg?
Is this a funny or serious moment in the play?
Give a reason for your answer.

99. "…Satan hasn't many have killed their da in Kerry, and in Mayo too."
Is Christy proud of himself in your view?
Is Christy entirely serious here, do you think?

100. Comment on Mahon arriving "on all fours" in the shebeen.
How would you expect the audience to react to this?

101. How does seeing Christy being taken for hanging make you feel?
Comment on the emotional impact of this scene.

102. What does Mahon's arrival mean for Christy?

103. Are you surprised that Pegeen burns Christy?
Is this a cruel thing to do?

Can you explain why she does this?
Would you do the same, in her position?

104. What does the way the locals treat Christy tell you about their world, their values and attitudes?

105. How do the locals react to seeing Mahon?
Explain their reaction.

106. How does Christy react to seeing his father?
What does this tell you about Christy's character?

107. What does Mahon do when he realises they are taking Christy to be hanged?
Does this surprise you?
Give a reason for your answer.

108. What excuse does Michael James give Mahon for how they have treated Christy?
Comment on his words here and what they reveal about his attitudes, beliefs and values.

109. What view does Mahon have of the people of Mayo, based on his experience?
Are his views justified, in your view?

110. How will things between him and his father be in future, according to Christy?
Does this surprise you?
Are you surprised that they are leaving together?
Give a reason for your answer.

111. What does Mahon say before he leaves the shebeen?
What does this tell you about him?

112. What are Christy's parting words?
What do they mean?
What does this tell you about Christy?

113. What does Michael James say when Christy and Mahon leave?
Are things returning to normal?
Is this a good or a bad thing for the characters?

114. What are Shawn Keogh's thoughts of, now that Christy is gone?
What is your response to this?

115. How does Pegeen react to Shawn here?
Are you surprised by her behaviour?

116. Why is Pegeen overcome as the play ends?
What is your response to this?
Do you feel sorry for Pegeen Mike?

117. The Widow Quin never returns with the doctor.
Why, do you think, is this the case?
Why, do you think, did the playwright write her exit this way?
Did she help Christy more than anyone else?
Did the Widow Quin care about Christy?

118. Is the action of Act Three ridiculous and comical or serious and provocative?

Refer to the text to support your viewpoint.
What is your response to the action of this final act?

119. Do you like this ending?
Has a very dark outcome been narrowly avoided?
Comment on this.
Why has the playwright chosen to end it this way?
What point is he making?

120. Why do you think, did Irish theatre-goers riot when this play was first performed in 1907?
What made them take such offence?
Were they justified to react like this, in your view?
Give reasons for your answer.

121. Is this play a comedy? Why/why not?

122. How do you feel as the play ends?
Give a reason for your answer.

123. Will Pegeen Mike marry Shawn Keogh, do you think?
Refer to the text to support your point of view.

124. Does this play depict a real or imagined Ireland?
Give reasons for your answer.

Further Questions

1. Did you enjoy the ending of this play? Why/why not?
   What questions are you left with?

2. Comment on the fact that Christy leaves with his father.

3. Do the characters in 'The Playboy of the Western World' lead happy lives?
   Refer to the text to support your views.

4. Why is Pegeen in tears at the end of the play?
   Do you feel sorry for her?

5. How do you imagine life for Christy in the future?
   How do you imagine life for Pegeen Mike in the future?
   Who will be happiest, in your view?

6. Is the Widow Quin a manipulative character?
   How does this affect the storyline?
   How do her actions affect the play's tone and outlook?
   Is she a warm or cold character?
   What does this add to the play?

7. Theatre-goers rioted in Dublin in 1907 when this play was first performed.
   Can you explain how the play provoked this response?

8. Did you become emotionally involved in this story?
   Why is this the case?

9. Do you like how this story is told?

10. How is family life portrayed in this play?
    Is this a realistic picture of family relationships, do you think?
    Does this picture of family life still ring true today?
    Refer to the text to support your ideas.

11. Who is your favourite character in this play?
    What do you like about them?

12. Who is your least favourite character in this play?
    What do you dislike about them?

13. What are the major themes and issues in this text?
    How are they explored?
    What conclusions do you draw?

14. Does this story teach us anything about people?
    Does it teach us anything about life?
    Refer to the text to support the points you make.

15. What is important to the characters in this text?
    How does this make you feel about them?

16. What did you enjoy about this story?

17. What did you dislike about this story?

18. Is this play engaging and entertaining? Explain your point of view.

19. Is there darkness and menace in this play?
Where do you see it?
Is there humour and playfulness in this play?
Where do you see it?
Is this a serious drama, or a comedy, in your view?

20. Does this play remind you of any novels you have read, or plays or films you have seen?
Explain your point of view, including examples to support your view.

Theme/Issue (HL)/Relationships (OL)

Relationships has been selected as the theme/issue to explore in relation to this text.

The theme of relationships can be applied to any relationship in a text and includes love, marriage, friendship and family bonds. Consider the complexities of relationships and the impact they have on characters' lives.

1. What is Pegeen's relationship to Shawn Keogh?
   As the play begins, do they strike you as a couple in love?

2. In Act One, how does Pegeen Mike react when the Widow Quin tells Christy that Pegeen and Shawn are to wed?
   What does this suggest about their relationship?

3. Based on what you see throughout the play, does Pegeen care about Shawn?
   Does Shawn care about Pegeen?
   Do they get on well and have a good relationship?
   Is this a positive portrayal of a young couple who are to be wed?
   Give reasons for your answer.

4. Why did Christy kill his father?
   How did he do it?
   What do these details suggest about their relationship?

5. Does Christy show any guilt or remorse for killing his father?
What does this suggest about their relationship?

6. Why does Mahon come to find Christy?

7. How does Mahon view his son?
What does this tell you about their relationship?

8. How does Christy feel about his father being alive?
How do these details add to your view of Christy's relationship with his father?

9. What made Christy attack his father for a second time, in Act Three?
What does this suggest about their relationship?
What is your response to Christy's actions here?

10. Do Christy and his father resolve their differences by the end of the play?
Why do they leave together at the end?
What does this suggest about their relationship?

11. Was Mahon a good father to Christy?
Was Christy a good son?
Give reasons for your answers.

12. Do Christy and his father communicate well?
Refer to the text to support your view.
What weaknesses do you see in their relationship?
What strengths do you see in their relationship?

13. Describe Christy's relationship with his father, based on what you learn of them throughout the play
   Use examples to support the points you make.

14. Do Pegeen Mike and the Widow Quin have a friendly or hostile relationship?
   Can you explain why they feel like this about one another?
   What does their relationship add to the theme of relationships as a whole?

15. How does the Widow Quin manipulate Shawn?
   Does she manipulate other characters?
   What does this add to the theme of relationships?

16. What makes Christy attractive in Pegeen Mike's eyes?
   Is this a good basis for a relationship, do you think?

17. What makes Pegeen Mike attractive in Christy's eyes?
   Is this a good basis for a relationship, do you think?

18. In Act Two, how does Pegeen scare and manipulate Christy?
   Why does she do this?

19. Are Pegeen and Christy happy and hopeful as they plan their marriage in Act Three?
   Are they loving towards one another?
   Do they value one another?
   Do they communicate well?
   Would theirs be an equal partnership, in your view?
   Refer to the text to support your point of view.

CLASSROOM QUESTIONS

20. What causes Pegeen to turn on Christy?
    What is your response to her behaviour here?
    How does she treat Christy once his father appears?
    Comment on her actions and words once she learns his father lives.
    Is Christy steadfast in his feelings for Pegeen?

21. Did Pegeen Mike and Christy really care about each other, in your view?
    Can you explain why their relationship failed?

22. What strengths do you see in Pegeen and Christy's relationship?
    What weaknesses do you see in Pegeen and Christy's relationship?
    Could they have been happy together, do you think?

23. What does the failure of their relationship add to the theme of relationships in this text?

24. Do characters in this text care about each other?
    Use examples to explain your stance.

25. Do characters in this text have a realistic view of love?
    Explain, using examples from the text to support the points you make.

26. Are characters in this play isolated from one another and lonely, do you think?

27. Does conflict characterise relationships in this play or do characters get on well?

28. What else characterises relationships in this text? (Are they generally supportive, secretive, honest, loving, etc.?)

29. What makes characters behave as they do in their relationships with one another?

30. Are their relationships a source of happiness for these characters?
Explain your point of view.

31. What is the most significant relationship in this story?
What makes this relationship stand out for you?
What does it tell us about human relationships, friendship and love?

32. Are relationships in this story positive or negative?
Are they meaningful or shallow?
What makes them this way?

33. Do relationships in this story bring characters happiness or sorrow?
Include examples in your answer.

34. What makes relationships difficult in this text?

35. What helps relationships in this text?

36. How do relationships change during the story?

37. What do you learn about relationships from studying this play?

38. Are relationships portrayed realistically in this text? Make use of examples to support the points that you make.

39. Are relationships in this story interesting and involving? Explain your point of view, using examples to illustrate your ideas.

40. Does any aspect of the theme of relationships in this text shock, upset or unsettle you?
Use examples to help explain your point of view.

Cultural Context (HL)/Social Setting (OL)

*Cultural Context/Social Setting refers to the world of the text.
Consider social norms, beliefs, values and attitudes.*

1. What does the setting of the play tell you about the world of the characters?
   Be specific in your answer.

2. When we first meet Shawn Keogh he says he and Pegeen have made a "good bargain" and are waiting on "dispensation from the bishops, or the Court of Rome" so they can marry.
   What do these details tell you about marriage in this world?

3. In his opening conversation with Pegeen, Shawn says he passed a man groaning in the furzy ditch, but did not stop to help him.
   What does this reveal about this place?

4. Based on the opening of Act One, how do you know that the Church is a powerful influence in these characters' lives?

5. When Christy Mahon enters the shebeen and asks about the police, the others wonder what crime he has committed.
What does the nature of his imagined crimes reveal about this place?

6. How do the others respond to Christy's story of murdering his father?
Do their reactions surprise you?
What do their responses reveal about their world?

7. What is a 'wake'?
What does it tell you about the setting here?

8. In Act One, Christy tells Pegeen what his homeplace was like.
What stands out for you about his home?

9. In Act One, the knock at the door frightens Christy as he is afraid of "the peelers, and the walking dead."
What do his fears tell you about this world?

10. In Act One the Widow Quin comes to fetch Christy Mahon to lodge with her.
Why does the priest think it is wrong for Christy to stay with Pegeen Mike?
What does this reveal about this world?

11. The Widow Quin struck her husband with a pick, but is walking free.
What do these details suggest about this world?

12. In Act Two Pegeen describes what would happen to a man that destroyed his da.
Outline this treatment.
What insight does this give you into the justice system of this world?

13. How do you know they live in a rural setting?
List your points and refer to the text in your answer.

14. In Act Two, the Widow Quin suggests a bargain to Shawn if she marries Christy.
What do these negotiations reveal about this world and what these characters value?

15. Why do the locals respect and admire Christy Mahon?
What great qualities does he possess?
What does this reveal to you about this world?

16. Why are Michael James and Pegeen so keen to hand Christy over for hanging at the end of Act Three?
What does this tell you about law and justice in this world?

17. Why isn't it murder to hang Christy?
Comment on this mindset.

18. What attitude do the locals have towards murder when Christy first arrives?
What does this tell you about this place?
How does their attitude change with Mahon's arrival?
What does this tell you about this place?

19. Christy is tortured(burned with a lighted sod) as the villagers try to drag him out for hanging.
Is this a barbaric act?
Is Christy treated cruelly here?
Is he treated justly?
What does the treatment of Christy, following his second attempt on his father's life, reveal about this world?

20. At the end of the play, Shawn speaks again of marrying Pegeen.
What does their relationship reveal to you about the world of this play?

21. Is theirs a very religious world?
Give reasons for your answer.

22. Are they superstitious people?
Give reasons for your answer.

23. Are characters' views traditional and conservative or modern and liberal?
Refer to the text to support your ideas.

24. What time and place is this story set in?

25. Is this world a romantic or practical place?
Explain your point of view.

26. Are wealth and class important in this world?
What view do characters have towards money and class?

27. Is race important in this world?

28. Are characters in this text moral and upstanding?

29. What do characters value in this story?

30. What kind of society do you see in this text?
    (How do people treat one another? What do they believe in? What is important to them?)

31. Is there violence and conflict in this world?
    Where do you see this violence and conflict?

32. Is this a secure or dangerous world?

33. What is the role of women in the world of this play?

34. How are women viewed and treated in this story?

35. Is family important in the world of this text?

36. What is the most important thing to characters in this world?
    What is your response to this?

37. Are characters in this world free to live as they choose, or must they conform to society's expectations?

38. Is this world a supportive or destructive environment for the play's characters?

39. Is the world of this text a joyful or dreary place?
    Use examples to justify your viewpoint.

40. Are friendship and love important in this world, or are characters self-centred and self-serving?
Justify your viewpoint with reference to the text.

41. Is their world a warm, loving place, or a cold, unfeeling place?
Justify your viewpoint with reference to the text.

42. Would you like to live in the world of 'The Playboy of the Western World'?
Include examples to justify your viewpoint.

43. How is the world of 'The Playboy of the Western World' similar to your world?
How is it different?
Use examples to support your point of view.

Literary Genre (HL)

Literary Genre refers to the way the story is told. Consider aspects of narration such as the manner and style of narration, characterisation, setting, tension, literary techniques, etc.

1. How does the play's opening arouse your interest and curiosity?

2. How does the wake in the background add to the atmosphere and setting in the first act?

3. How does Christy Mahon's arrival in Act One contribute to the story?

4. How does the arrival of the Widow Quin in Act One act as a source of conflict in the play?

5. Does a lot happen in the opening scene?
   What is the purpose of this opening scene?

6. Does Shawn Keogh act as a potential source of conflict? Explain your point of view.
   What other functions does Shawn's character serve?

7. What is your reaction to the Widow Quin's bargain with Shawn, that she will marry Christy?

Is this an exciting moment in the play?
If so, what makes it exciting?

8. Mahon, Christy's injured father, comes looking for him towards the end of Act Two.
How does this development enhance the story?
Does Mahon pose a threat to Christy?
Give reasons for your answer.

9. How does Michael James' return to the shebeen further the plot?

10. How does the playwright manipulate the audience emotionally throughout this play?
How does he get our hopes up?
How does he play on our anticipation?
How does he use pacing to good effect to make us invest ourselves in the events of the play?

11. How important is anticipation as a device for involving the audience in this play?
Make use of specific examples in your answer.

12. Is the ending of this play violent and cruel?
How does it add to the story?

13. What is Synge communicating to the audience through his characters' actions?

14. Mahon lives a second time.
Is this a clever twist or a cheat?
Did you see this coming?

Why has Synge included this turn of events, do you think?
How does it affect the story?

15. What impact does Mahon's arrival at the end have on the audience?

16. Mahon's arrival at the end of the play is not explained. Does this matter?
Does it help or hinder the storytelling in your view?
Give reasons for your answer.

17. The Widow Quin goes to fetch the doctor to save Christy, but does not return.
What is Synge doing here?
How does he manipulate his audience here?

18. Is Christy a complex character?
Is he an attractive or repellent character?
Include specific details in your answer.

19. How does the writer make this story increasingly tense and exciting?
Be specific in your answer.

20. How are characters in this play depicted?
Generally, are characters to be admired or criticised?
Explain your point of view.
What does this add to the story?

21. How are men and women depicted in this play?
    What is the effect of this?
    How does this contribute to the story?

22. How does setting contribute to the story?

23. Do you find this play to be interesting and easy to follow?

24. What draws the audience into this story?
    Highlight specific aspects of the the text in your answer.

25. How does the playwright create a darker, sinister edge to the story at times?

26. Identify the various sources of conflict in this text.
    How does the use of conflict add to this story?

27. What does violence add to the story?

28. Does this play have a satisfying ending? Explain your point of view.

29. Comment on the mood as the story ends.

30. Did you enjoy this story?
    Use examples from the text to support your answer.

31. Who is your favourite character in this play?
    What makes you like/admire them?

32. Who is your least favourite character in this play?
    What makes you dislike them?

33. Is this story told well, in your view?
    Give reasons for your answer, referring to the play to support your ideas.

34. Do you enjoy the role that coincidence plays in the story?

35. What draws the audience into this story?
    Highlight specific aspects of the text in your answer.

36. What are the high points of this play?
    What makes them exciting and intriguing?

37. Did you enjoy the storyline of the text?
    Was it exciting, compelling, tense or emotional?
    Use examples from the text to support your answer.

38. Is there just one plot or many plots?
    What connections can you make between these storylines?

39. What interested you most in the story?

40. Are characters vivid, realistic and well-developed?
    Explain your point of view, using examples from the text.

41. Do you empathise or identify with any characters?

42. What themes can you identify in this story?

43. Is this a comedy?
    Explain your viewpoint.

44. How does the playwright create suspense, high emotion and excitement in this text?
What techniques does he use to good advantage?

45. Consider the author's use of tension and resolution in the play.
What are the major tensions/problems/conflicts in the text?
Are they resolved or not?

46. Does the playwright make use of any striking patterns of imagery or symbols to add to this story?

47. How does the playwright make use of the unexpected?
What does this add to the story?

48. What is the climax (high point) of the story?
What do you think of this moment?
How does it make you feel?

49. Comment on the language of the play.
How does dialogue and dialect add to the story?

50. What do you find moving or emotional in this play?

51. What aspects of the play form worked well in this story, in your view?

52. What do you like about the way this story is told?

53. To what genre does this play belong?
Support your choice with examples from the text.

General Vision and Viewpoint (HL)

General Vision and Viewpoint refers to the author's outlook or view of life and how this viewpoint is represented in the text.

1. How does the playwright create a sense of threat or menace as the play begins?
   Refer to specific details in your answer.

2. As the play opens, Pegeen Mike is concerned about spending the night alone.
   How do her fears add to the mood and General Vision and Viewpoint here?

3. There is talk of a man dying in a ditch as the play begins, but no mention of going to help him.
   How does this colour the mood of the opening of the play?

4. When he reveals his crime, Christy says he murdered his father for being dirty and old.
   How does this affect the General Vision and Viewpoint of the play?

5. The locals in the shebeen are impressed to hear of Christy's murder of his father.
   Comment on their outlook here.

CLASSROOM QUESTIONS • 75

> Is this a very cold response?
> What is your response to this worldview?

6. Christy tells us, "Up to the day I killed my father, there wasn't a person in Ireland knew the kind I was…"
   How does Christy feel about himself here?
   What is your response to this sentiment?
   What does it suggest about life?

7. Christy Mahon's status as murderer earns him admiration from the play's other characters.
   Comment on this outlook.

8. As Act Two begins, four local girls bring Christy gifts of food, to help sustain him after killing his father.
   What is the playwright revealing about human nature and life here?

9. How does Pegeen's talk of hanging affect the atmosphere in Act Two?

10. In Act Two, Christy talks of leaving and how lonesome he is, walking past towns at night.
    How does his loneliness and the imagery he uses add to the atmosphere?

11. What does the Widow Quin's bargain with Shawn about marrying Christy reveal to you about her outlook?
    Do you feel good about the deal she strikes here?
    Why/why not?
    Is she manipulating Shawn here?
    What is your response to this?

12. When Christy learns his father is alive, he gets angry. How does this contribute to the General Vision and Viewpoint of the play?

13. What do the Widow Quin's deals reveal about human nature?
    Is this a positive or negative aspect of our nature?

14. Read the Widow Quin's words at the end of Act Two. What do they mean?
    What do they suggest about life?

15. How well does Christy get on in the sports?
    How is he treated by the locals?
    Is he enjoying himself since he arrived here?
    What does Christy's experience in this place show you about people and life?

16. Do you feel optimistic about their future when Christy proposes to Pegeen in Act Three?
    Give a reason for your answer.

17. What makes the locals turn on Christy later on?
    Why does Christy find it difficult to accept this change?
    What does their treatment of Christy in the final stages reveal about human nature?
    Is Pegeen cruel to Christy here?

18. In Act Three, Christy is roped around the neck and threatened with scorching if he does not release his grip, so that he can be taken for hanging.
    Is this barbaric treatment of Christy?

Is he treated as a human being should be?
What makes the other characters degrade him like this?
What does this episode reveal about human nature?
Is this a positive or negative aspect of humanity?
What is the playwright demonstrating here?
How do you feel about the way Christy is treated here?

19. Why is Christy viewed as a romantic hero at first?
Can you explain the mindset of the locals?

20. Does the Widow Quin have a self-centred approach to life?
How does her manipulation, scheming and bargaining add to the General Vision and Viewpoint of the play?
Is she entirely self-centred?
Do the other characters share her approach to life?
What does her behaviour suggest about life?

21. Is Shawn Keogh a weak, fearful character?
Give a reason for your answer.
What does his behaviour suggest about life?
Do the other characters share his approach to life?
How is he treated by the others?
What does this tell you about human nature?

22. Is love doomed in this world? Explain your point of view.

23. Why does Pegeen's relationship with Christy fail?
Could it have been succesful, in this world?
How does the failure of their relationship contribute to the General Vision and Viewpoint of the play?

24. The characters in this play are drawn to Christy when they learn of his bloody deed.
Is it in our nature to be attracted to sensational and gory stories?
Is this the appeal that Christy holds for the locals?
What does this fascination with gruesome death suggest about human nature and life?

25. The Widow Quin tried to kill her husband. Christy tried to kill his father twice. How do their actions impact on the play's General Vision and Viewpoint?

26. Do characters in this play have a flippant attitude to murder?
How does this contribute to the General Vision and Viewpoint of the text?

27. As the play ends, whose future is bright and whose is bleak?
Why is this the case?
Are you happy with how things have turned out?

28. Do characters in this play deserve their endings?
Refer to the text to support your views.

29. Is this a violent play?
Are the characters violent people?
How does this contribute to the General Vision and Viewpoint of the play?

30. Are characters in this text hopeful and forward looking about life?

Are they realistic? Do they make well-thought out plans?
What does this suggest about their outlook in life?

31. What does this play suggest about human nature?
What does this suggest about human nature?
Is this outlook positive or negative?

32. Is there a lesson or moral to this story?
What could it be?
Does the play end on a hopeful or hopeless note?

33. Is life to be enjoyed or endured in the world of this text?
Refer to the play to support your ideas.
Explain your point of view.

34. What comments do characters make on their society and the problems they are facing?

35. Are characters happy or unhappy?

36. What makes characters in this story happy and fulfilled?

37. What makes characters in this story unhappy and unfulfilled?

38. Are relationships destructive or nurturing?
What do they reveal about life as we see characters supported/thwarted in their efforts to grow/mature?

39. Is life full of possibility and potential in this text?

40. Are imagery and language bright or dark in the text?
(Tone of the text)

41. What is the mood of this text?
    Include examples to justify your ideas.

42. What does this play suggest about human nature?
    Is this outlook positive or negative?

43. How does humour influence the General Vision and Viewpoint of this play?

44. Do characters face many obstacles and difficulties in this text? Do they struggle?
    Why/why not?

45. Is this text dark and bleak or uplifting and inspiring?
    Give reasons for your view.

46. Is there a lesson or moral to this story?
    What could it be?
    Does it still hold true today?

47. What does this story teach us about life?

48. How do you feel as you watch the play?
    Refer to key moments to anchor your answer.

49. Does the play end on a hopeful, optimistic note, or a hopeless, pessimistic one?
    Are questions raised by the text resolved by the end?
    Are they resolved happily or unhappily?
    How do you feel at the end?
    Explain your point of view.

50. Are you hopeful or despairing regarding the prospects for human happiness in this story?
(Are characters likely to be happy?)

51. Identify the aspects of life that the playwright concentrates on.
Are they positive or negative?
What is he telling us by focusing on these aspects of life?

52. Identify bright, hopeful, optimistic aspects of the play.

53. Identify dark, hopeless, pessimistic aspects of the play.

54. Does this play offer a comforting or disturbing view of life?
Overall, is it optimistic or pessimistic?
Explain your point of view.

Hero, Heroine, Villain (OL)

'Hero, Heroine, Villain' refers to central characters (protagonists/antagonists).

Their traits, values, etc. and their ability to deal with conflict, challenges, obstacles, etc. should be considered.

Christy Mahon

1. What are your first impressions of Christy when he enters the shebeen?

2. How did he kill his father?
   What is your response to this?

3. Does he seem sorry for killing his father?
   What is your response to this?
   How does this affect your view of him?

4. Is Christy presented as a 'typical' murderer?
   Explain your ideas fully here.

5. Is Christy what you might expect a murderer to be like?
   Give reasons for your answer.

6. Is Christy a likeable character?
   Give reasons for your answer.

7. Is Christy selfish and self-centred or kind and generous?
   Refer to the text to support the points you make.

8. Is he a proud or modest man?

9. Is Christy a violent man?
   Would you be afraid of him if you met him?
   Why/why not?

10. What sort of life has Christy had?
    How has this affected him as a person?

11. Does Christy lie to Pegeen?
    What does this tell you about him?
    What is your response to this?

12. Does Christy love Pegeen?
    How does this affect your view of him?

13. Does Christy lead on the Widow Quin?
    What does this tell you about him?
    How does this affect your view of him?

14. What makes Christy attack his father the second time?
    What does this tell you about him?

15. Why doesn't Christy run away when the Widow Quin and Sara tell him to in Act Three?
    What does this tell you about Christy?

16. Is Christy faced with a lot of challenges and problems in the play?
How does he deal with these challenges and problems?
What is your response to this?

17. Is Christy really a murderer?
How do you feel about the crimes he has committed?

18. Do you like Christy Mahon?
What makes you feel this way about him?
Are you happy with the way things have turned out for him?

19. Choose three words that sum up Christy for you.
Give reasons for your choices, referring to specific instances in the play in your answer.

20. If you could chat to Christy, what would you talk about?
What advice would you give him?
What questions would you ask?

The Comparative Study: Comparing Texts

Use the following questions to compare your texts, noting the similarities and differences between them. Include examples to support the points that you make.

Theme/Issue - Relationships

1. Are relationships in this text more positive and supportive than the relationships in your other chosen texts?
   Include specific examples in your answer.

2. Rank the relationships you have studied in your various texts from most positive (score of 10) to most negative (score of 1).
   Add a note explaining your choices.

3. Are relationships in this text the most engaging and interesting that you have studied?
   Explain your choice.

4. Rank the relationships you have studied in your various texts from the most interesting (score of 10) to the least

interesting (score of 1).
Add a note explaining your choices.

5. Did you learn most about the theme of relationships from this text or another text on your Comparative Study course?
Refer to your chosen texts to support your answer.

6. What similarities do you notice in the theme of relationships in this text and your other Comparative Study texts?

7. What differences do you notice in the theme of relationships in this text and your other Comparative Study texts?

8. How do the events of the text impact on the characters' relationships with one another in this text and your other chosen texts?
Who is most affected?
Who is least affected?

9. How does conflict impact on the relationships of characters in this text and other chosen texts?
Who is most affected?
Who is least affected?

10. How does social class impact on the relationships of characters in this text and other chosen texts?
Who is most affected?
Who is least affected?

11. Is the theme of relationships portrayed in an idealistic or realistic way in each of your chosen texts?

12. Did any aspect of the theme of relationships shock or surprise you in your three chosen texts?
    Use examples from your texts to support the points that you make.

13. What are the most interesting aspects of the theme of relationships in each of your chosen texts?

14. Which text taught you most about relationships?
    Refer to each text in your answer.

15. Which key moments best capture the theme of relationships in each of your texts?

16. What similarities do you notice in the theme of relationships in this text and your other comparative study texts?

17. What differences do you notice in the theme of relationships in this text and your other Comparative Study texts?

Literary Genre

1. Did you like the way this story was told more than your other comparative texts?
   State what you enjoyed most (and least) about each.

2. Is this text more exciting than your other texts?
   Consider tension, suspense, pacing, conflict and the author's use of the unexpected.

3. How does the author make use of tension in each of your chosen texts?
   Where is it most effective?
   Where is it least effective?
   Use examples to support your point of view.

4. How does the author make use of climax in each of your chosen texts?
   Where is it most effective?
   Where is it least effective?
   Use examples to support your point of view.

5. How does the author make use of resolution in each of your chosen texts?
   Where is it most effective?
   Where is it least effective?
   Use examples to support your point of view.

6. Are characters more engaging in this text than in your other texts?
Refer to each of your texts in your answer.

7. How does the author create vivid, memorable characters in each of your chosen texts?

8. In which of your texts are characters most life-like and compelling?
In which text are characters least life-like and most difficult to relate to?
Refer to each of your texts in your answer.

9. Is the setting more effective in telling the story in this text, than in your other texts?

10. Is this text more unpredictable than your other texts?
Refer to each of your texts in your answer.

11. Does this text have greater emotional power than your other texts?
Was this emotional power created in a more interesting way here or in a different text?
Refer to each of your texts in your answer.

12. What was your favourite literary technique, used by the author of each of your texts?
How did the use of this technique help the storytelling?

13. To what extent are you influenced by the point of view that this story is told from?
Are you influenced to a greater or lesser degree by the

point of view utilised in your other Comparative Study texts?

14. Which key moments best capture Literary Genre in each of your texts?

15. What similarities do you notice in the Literary Genre of this text and your other Comparative Study texts? Mention specific aspects of narrative.

16. What differences do you notice in the Literary Genre of this text and your other Comparative Study texts? Mention specific aspects of narrative.

General Vision and Viewpoint

1. Is life happier and fuller for characters in this text than in your other Comparative Study texts?
Explain your point of view fully.

2. Do characters in this text face more obstacles and difficulties than in your other texts?
Who struggles most?

3. Are characters in this text rewarded more for their struggles than in your other texts?
Do they overcome adversity and achieve true happiness and contentment in a way that is not realised in your other texts?

4. How do events in these texts, and your personal response to these events, help your understanding of the General Vision and Viewpoint of these texts?
Include specific examples in your answer.

5. How does your attitude to central characters help shape your understanding of the General Vision and Viewpoint of your chosen texts?
Include specific reference to your chosen characters in your answer.

6. What aspects of this text did you respond to emotionally? How does this help your understanding of the General Vision and Viewpoint of the text?
How does this compare to your other texts?

7. Is this the brightest, most hopeful and triumphant text you have studied?
Explain why its message is more or less positive than in your other texts.

8. Which of your chosen texts was the bleakest and most upsetting or depressing?
Explain what made it more negative than your other texts. What made them more positive?

9. Plot your three texts on a scale of one to ten from darkest (most pessimistic) to brightest (most optimistic). Add a note to explain their positions.

10. Which key moments best capture the General Vision and Viewpoint of each of your texts?

11. What similarities do you notice in the General Vision and Viewpoint of this text and your other Comparative Study texts?

12. Which differences do you notice in the General Vision and Viewpoint of this text and your other Comparative Study texts?

13. Can you relate any aspect of this text to your own life experience?
    If so, how does this help to shape your understanding of the General Vision and Viewpoint of this text?

Cultural Context/Social Setting

Consider each of your chosen texts in your answers.

1. In which of the texts you have studied for the Comparative Study do characters have the most freedom and choice?
   Why is this the case?
   Justify your answer with examples from your chosen texts.

2. In which of your texts are characters most controlled?

3. Who holds the power in each world?
   Who is powerless?

4. In which world is difference most accepted and respected?
   In which world is difference least accepted and respected?

5. Which world is the least tolerant?
   Which world is the most tolerant?
   Include examples to explain your view.

6. Which world is the best to live in if you are a woman?
   Give reasons for your answer.

7. Which world is the best to live in if you are a man?
   Give reasons for your answer.

8. Which world is the best to live in if you are a child?
   Give reasons for your answer.

9. Which text portrays the most violent and volatile world?

10. Which of your texts portrays the safest, most secure place?

11. Which of your texts portrays the most supportive world?

12. Which of these worlds is the darkest, most fearful place?

13. Which of these worlds is the brightest, most joyful place?

14. Which of these places is the most unpredictable?

15. Which text portrays the most traditional world?

16. Which of these societies holds family in the highest esteem?

17. Which of these societies holds love in the highest esteem?
    Which of these societies holds love in the lowest esteem?

18. Which of these societies holds religion in the highest esteem?
    Which of these societies holds religion in the lowest esteem?

19. Which of these societies holds power in the highest esteem?

20. Which of these societies holds wealth in the highest esteem?

21. Where do you see the best treatment of the vulnerable of society? Include examples to support your view.

22. Where do you see the worst treatment of the vulnerable of society? Include examples to support your view.

23. Which of the worlds you have studied is the most materialistic?
    Which of the worlds you have studied is the least materialistic?
    What makes characters have these outlooks?

24. Which of the worlds you have studied is the most secretive?
    What makes characters behave this way?

25. Which of your texts displays the greediest world?
    What makes characters have this attitude?

26. Where is love most important?
    Where is love most successful?
    Where is love least important?
    Where is love least succesful?
    Compare the success of love in each of your chosen texts. What does this tell you about the worlds of these texts and characters' lives?

27. Which of these worlds appealed to you most?
    Give reasons for your answer.

28. Which of these worlds appealed to you least?
    Explain your point of view.

29. Which of your texts is home to the most religious or spiritual world?

30. Which of your texts showed the least religious or spiritual society?

31. How important is social class in each of your texts?

32. In which of your texts are characters most accepting of their world and society?

33. In which of your texts do characters challenge their world, society and values most?

34. In which of your texts do you see the greatest inequality?

35. In which of your texts do you see the greatest injustice?

36. Where do characters behave the best towards one another?
    How does Cultural Context/Social Setting influence their behaviour?

37. How do characters reflect the Cultural Context/Social Setting of their worlds?
    Explain, including examples.

38. How does the Cultural Context/Social Setting of your texts lead to problems and difficulties for the texts' characters?
    How does it affect characters' responses to these difficulties?

39. Which key moments best capture the Cultural Context/Social Setting of each of your texts?

40. What similarities do you notice in the Cultural Context/Social Setting of this text and your other Comparative Study texts?

41. What differences do you notice in the Cultural Context/Social Setting of this text and your other Comparative Study texts?

Hero/Heroine/Villain

Consider the following list of questions for a central character in each of your chosen texts.

1. Who is the most interesting character in the text?
   What makes them interesting?
   What do you like about them?
   What do you dislike about them?
   What are this character's strengths?
   What are this character's weaknesses?

2. How does this character cope with conflict?

3. How does this character cope with the unexpected?

4. Are they a resourceful character?

5. Are they an emotional character?
   Use examples to support your view.

6. Do you empathise with this character? Why/why not?

7. What do you admire about this character?

8. How well does this character relate to and interact with other characters?
   Include examples to support your points.

9. Is this character happy or sad?

10. Are they an active or passive character?
    How do they contribute to the action and storyline of the text?
    Are they important to the story's plot and development?

11. Is this character a good (successful and interesting) main character?

12. Would you like to meet this character?
    If you met them, what would you talk about?

13. If you had any advice for this character, what would it be?

14. Does this character make the story more exciting?
    In what way do they do this?

15. Is this character a hero/heroine or a villain?
    Explain your choice.

16. Identify the key moments in the text that illustrate your chosen character's personality traits/character.

17. On a scale of one to ten (with one being extremely heroic and ten being an evil villain), where would you place your chosen character?
    Give reasons for your choice.
    Where would you place the main characters from your other texts?
    Why would you place them here?

18. Which of your chosen characters do you like and admire most?

What makes them your favourite character?
Give reasons for your answer.

19. Which of your chosen characters do you dislike most?
Explain why you like some more than others.

20. Which of your chosen characters shocked you most?
Give reasons for your answer.

21. Which of your chosen characters impressed you most?
Give reasons for your answer.

22. Which of your chosen characters did you feel most sorry for?
Give reasons for your answer.

23. Who is the most resourceful character you have come across?
Give reasons for your answer.

24. Which of your chosen characters faced the most problems and difficulties?
Did they cope well with these problems?

25. How is your favourite character similar to the characters in your other texts?

26. How is your favourite character different to the characters in your other texts?

27. Choose key moments from each of your texts to highlight your characters' strengths and weaknesses.

www.ingramcontent.com/pod-product-compliance
Lightning Source LLC
Chambersburg PA
CBHW071018080526
44587CB00015B/2421